GINGERBREAD
HOUSES, ANIMALS AND DECORATIONS

Explore the delicious versatility of
gingerbread in 24 delightful projects

Joanna Farrow

LORENZ BOOKS

This edition is published by Lorenz Books,
an imprint of Anness Publishing Ltd,
Blaby Road, Wigston, Leicestershire
LE18 4SE; info@anness.com

www.lorenzbooks.com;
www.annesspublishing.com

If you like the images in this book and would like to investigate using them for publishing, promotions or advertising, please visit our website www.practicalpictures.com for more information.

Publisher: Joanna Lorenz
Editorial Director: Helen Sudell
Designer: Bobbie Colgate Stone
Photographer and Stylist: Michelle Garrett
Home Economist: Joanna Farrow, assisted by Julie Beresford
Illustrator: Lucinda Ganderton

A CIP catalogue record for this book is available from the British Library.

Previously published as *A Little Book of Gingerbread*

PUBLISHER'S NOTE
Although the advice and information in this book are believed to be accurate and true at the time of going to press, neither the authors nor the publisher can accept any legal responsibility or liability for any errors or omissions that may have been made nor for any inaccuracies nor for any loss, harm or injury that comes about from following instructions or advice in this book.

Templates
Some of the templates at the back of the book will need scaling up to the required size. If you have access to a photocopier it will do the job for you. Otherwise, copy the template on to tracing paper, draw a squared grid over it, and transfer the template, square by square, on to a sheet of larger scale graph paper.

CONTENTS

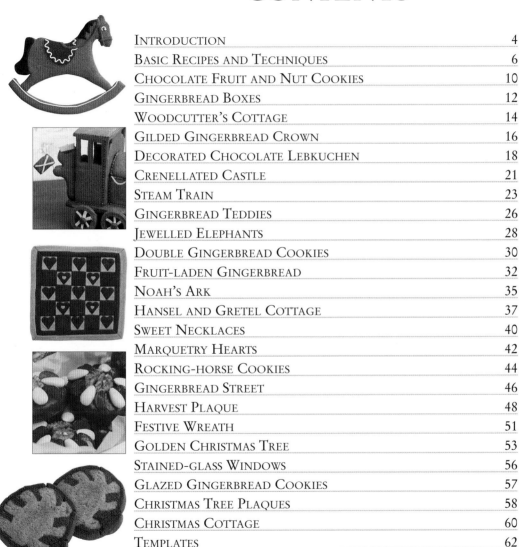

INTRODUCTION

ONE OF THE MOST ANCIENT of spices, ginger has been traded across the world for centuries, resulting in a wonderful array of uses, especially as a flavouring for sweet cakes and cookies. Ornately decorated festive houses, spiced fruit cakes, yeasted sweet loaves and teabreads, chunky cookies and moist, sticky cakes, can all be accurately described as 'gingerbread'.

All the different types of ginger available come from fresh root ginger, a fibrous, woody root, which can be used freshly grated in both sweet and savoury dishes. In gingerbread, it is usually the dried and ground root, sold as a powder, that gives the spicy flavour. Stem, crystallized and glacé (candied) ginger, and all forms of preserved young root ginger can also be chopped and added to cakes, cookies, breads, fillings and icings.

♥ *Sturdy metal cutters are perfect for shaping gingerbread hearts.*

This book demonstrates the decorative value of cooking gingerbread. This is a technique that developed during the last century, as gingerbread became increasingly popular in Europe. In medieval Europe, when fairs were widely enjoyed, gingerbread would be sold in pretty shapes, often gilded and studded with spices. Fairs became known as 'Gingerbread Fairs' and fair-goers would buy gingerbread for gifts or 'fairings'.

Nuremberg in Germany became known as the 'Gingerbread Capital' of the world, because of its central position on the northern trade routes. Here, the art of making gingerbread moulds to shape ornate gingerbread carvings was developed. These were made into the shapes of kings and queens, windmills, letters, hearts and animals. When baked and turned out, these elaborate shapes were frequently gilded with gold paint and sold at markets and fairs.

The German fairy tale 'Hansel and Gretel', in which the children discover a house made entirely of gingerbread, sweets (candies) and cake, inspired the trend for making beautiful constructions based on gingerbread. These often have a 'fairy-tale' appearance, prettily dusted with sugar and traditionally presented to friends at Christmas.

Today, most people associate gingerbread with Christmas but there are many other times of year when it makes a delicious gift or simply a creative treat for all the family. A cleverly constructed castle, train or cottage makes an impressive birthday cake for children and the young at heart. Decorative gingerbread cookies also make lovely gifts, wrapped in tissue and presented in an ornate box or tin with ribbon decoration.

WORKING WITH GINGERBREAD

There are several points to remember when working with gingerbread for the first time. You might find it easier to shape large, cut-out pieces of gingerbread on the baking sheet, so that the dough doesn't distort as you transfer it from the work surface. Unless the recipe instructs otherwise, space the gingerbread slightly apart on the baking sheet, to allow room for expansion.

Like any biscuit, gingerbread is not crisp or firm when it first comes out of the oven; this means it can be difficult to tell whether it is cooked, particularly as cooking times vary from oven to oven. Generally, the biscuit will have risen slightly and will just be colouring around the edges. Leave it on the baking sheet for a few minutes, in which time it will start to crisp. (If the gingerbread still feels very soft, return it to the oven for a few minutes.) Very often, the gingerbread will distort slightly during baking, but you can easily trim it once it is cooked.

Large, flat pieces of gingerbread must be cooled and stored on a flat surface or they will become distorted. For convenience, you may prefer to make the gingerbread a day before decorating it. If so, let it cool completely and then wrap it in baking parchment or cover it with clear film (plastic wrap).

♥ *These gingerbread cookies are made using an range of cutters and are decorated with ribbon and icing.*

BASIC RECIPES AND TECHNIQUES

*B*oth Golden Gingerbread and Chocolate Gingerbread are frequently used in this book, for
*shaping into buildings and other constructions, as they can be thinly rolled and have a firm
texture. Lebkuchen has a slightly softer texture, perfect for little and shaped cookies.
If using the dough for a recipe project, wrap and chill the gingerbread, and then refer to the project
for the shaping method. Alternatively, make simple cookies by cutting out shapes with a cutter and
baking them at 180°C/350°F/Gas 4 for about 12 minutes, until they are just beginning to colour
around the edges.*

GOLDEN GINGERBREAD

*175g/6oz/1½ cups plain
(all-purpose) flour
1.5ml/¼ tsp bicarbonate of soda
(baking soda)
a pinch of salt
5ml/1 tsp ground ginger
5ml/1 tsp ground cinnamon
60ml/4 tbsp unsalted butter, cubed
75g/3oz/6 tbsp caster (superfine) sugar
30ml/2 tbsp maple or golden
(light corn) syrup
1 egg yolk, beaten*

1 Sift together the flour, bicarbonate of soda, salt and spices. Rub the butter into the flour in a large bowl, until the mixture resembles fine breadcrumbs. Alternatively, blend in a food processor.

2 Add the sugar, syrup and egg yolk and mix or process to a firm dough. Knead lightly. Wrap and chill for 30 minutes before shaping.

CHOCOLATE GINGERBREAD

*175g/6oz/1½ cups plain
(all-purpose) flour
a pinch of salt
10ml/2 tsp mixed (apple pie) spice
2.5ml/½ tsp bicarbonate of soda
(baking soda)
25g/1oz/¼ cup unsweetened
cocoa powder
75g/3oz/6 tbsp unsalted
butter, cubed
75g/3oz/6 tbsp light muscovado
(brown) sugar
1 egg*

1 Sift together the flour, salt, spice, bicarbonate of soda and cocoa powder. Blend in a food processor, with the butter, until the mixture resembles fine breadcrumbs. Alternatively, knead the butter into the flour in a large bowl.

2 Add the sugar and egg and mix to a firm dough. Knead lightly. Wrap in clear film (plastic wrap) and chill for at least 30 minutes before shaping.

LEBKUCHEN

*115g/4oz/½ cup unsalted
butter, softened
115g/4oz/generous ½ cup light
muscovado (brown) sugar
1 egg, beaten
120ml/8 tbsp black treacle (molasses)
400g/14oz/3½ cups self-raising
(self-rising) flour
5ml/1 tsp ground ginger
2.5ml/½ tsp ground cloves
1.5ml/¼ tsp chilli powder*

1 Cream together the butter and sugar until pale and fluffy. Beat in the egg and black treacle. Sift the flour, ginger, cloves and chilli powder into the bowl. Using a wooden spoon, gradually mix the ingredients together to make a stiff paste. Turn out on to a lightly floured work surface and knead lightly until smooth. Wrap and chill for 30 minutes.

ICING GLAZE

This is like glacé icing but is thinned with egg white so that it sets.

*15ml/1 tbsp lightly beaten egg white
15ml/1 tbsp lemon juice
75–115g/3–4oz/⅔–1 cup icing
(confectioners') sugar*

♥ *Royal icing is ideal for piping decorations on to gingerbread.*

ROYAL ICING
The classic icing for gingerbread, this sets hard to give a good finish.

*1 egg white
200–225g/7–8oz/1⅔–2 cups icing
(confectioners') sugar*

1 Beat the egg white. Beat in the sugar, a little at a time, until the mixture is smooth and forms soft peaks. Transfer to a bowl and cover the surface with clear film (plastic wrap), to prevent a crust from forming. Store in the refrigerator for up to three days.

1 Mix the egg white and lemon juice in a bowl. Gradually beat in the icing sugar, until the mixture is smooth and has the consistency of thin cream. The icing should thinly coat the back of a spoon.

KNEADING COLOUR INTO SUGAR PASTE

You can buy coloured sugar paste from supermarkets and suppliers of cake-decorating equipment, but you might find it more convenient to buy a pack of white sugar paste and colour it as required. Paste food colours give the richest shades and are easier to use. Liquid colours can be used for pastel shades but they tend to make the paste quite soft.

1 Lightly knead the sugar paste on a surface dusted with icing (confectioners') sugar, to soften it. Dot the icing with a little paste food colouring, using a cocktail stick (toothpick). Knead in the colour to the required shade, adding more colour if necessary.

♥ *COOK'S TIP* ♥
If you don't want to use sugar paste straight away, wrap it in clear film (plastic wrap) and store it in a cool, dry place. Do not chill it or it will be difficult to work.

USING TEMPLATES

A number of the projects require a template made from designs at the back of the book, or a shape cut from paper following the directions in the project itself. Trace the template on to baking parchment and cut it out.

TRIMMING COOKED GINGERBREAD

When you are going to assemble gingerbread into a cottage, castle or any other construction requiring straight edges, you will usually need to trim the edges straight again after baking, to ensure that the pieces will fit accurately together. This is because the gingerbread will have spread and distorted slightly during the cooking process.

1 Once the the gingerbread is cool enough to handle, lay it on a flat surface or board. Using a serrated knife, cut through the gingerbread,

(You may prefer to copy the template on to thicker paper.)

1 Roll out the gingerbread dough and lay the template over it. Carefully cut around the template and transfer the gingerbread dough to a baking sheet.

with a gentle sawing action. It is a good idea to lightly hold the gingerbread down with the hand not doing the cutting, to prevent it moving around. If the original gingerbread shape has been cut using a template, lay the template over the cooked gingerbread and cut carefully around it.

MAKING A PAPER PIPING BAG

MELTING CHOCOLATE

1 Cut a 20cm/8in square of grease-proof (waxed) paper in half diagonally so that you have two triangles. Hold one triangle with the longest side away from you. Curl the left-hand point over to meet the point nearest you, to make a cone. Curl the right-hand point over the cone.

2 Bring the points neatly together, to make a neat cone. Fold the points over several times, to secure the bag.

1 Break the chocolate into pieces and put them in a small, heatproof bowl. Heat a small pan containing a little water to a very gentle simmer.

2 Place the bowl over the pan and leave the chocolate to melt. The base of the bowl should not touch the water or the chocolate will overheat. Stir gently and check that no lumps remain before using.

♥ COOK'S TIP ♥
One of the easiest ways to decorate gingerbread cookies is by using royal icing. Fill a paper piping bag with the royal icing, snip off the tip and drizzle on any design you choose.

♥ *Decorating cookies with white royal icing.*

CHOCOLATE FRUIT AND NUT COOKIES

These simple, chunky gingerbread cookies make a delicious gift, especially when presented in a decorative gift box. The combination of walnuts, almonds and cherries is very effective, but you can use any other mixture of fruits and nuts.

MAKES ABOUT 20
1 quantity Lebkuchen mixture
225g/8oz plain (semisweet) chocolate
50g/2oz/¼ cup caster (superfine) sugar
75ml/5 tbsp water
75g/3oz glacé (candied) cherries
40g/1½oz walnut halves
115g/4oz/⅔ cup whole blanched almonds

1 Preheat the oven to 180°C/350°F/ Gas 4. Grease two baking sheets. Shape the dough into a roll, 20cm/ 8in long. Chill for 30 minutes. Cut into 20 slices and space them on the baking sheets. Bake for 10 minutes. Leave on the baking sheets for 5 minutes and then transfer to a wire rack and leave to cool.

2 Break the chocolate into pieces. Put the sugar in a small, heavy pan with the water. Heat gently until the sugar dissolves. Bring to the boil and boil for 1 minute, until slightly syrupy. Leave for 3 minutes, to cool slightly, and then stir in the chocolate until it has melted and made a smooth sauce.

♥ *Carefully stack the cookies in a pretty box or tin, lined with tissue paper, or tie in cellophane bundles.*

3 Place the wire rack of cookies over a large tray or board to catch the drips. Spoon a little of the chocolate mixture over the cookies, spreading it to the edges with the back of the spoon.

4 Cut the glacé cherries into small wedges. Gently press a walnut half into the centre of each cookie. Arrange pieces of glacé cherry and almonds alternately around the nuts. Leave to set in a cool place.

♥ COOK'S TIP ♥
Store the cookies in an airtight tin until you are ready to eat them.

GINGERBREAD BOXES

F or chocolates or other edible gifts, these gingerbread boxes make lovely containers, giving you the opportunity to experiment with various decorative techniques, such as cut-outs and painting.

MAKES 1 LARGE AND 1 SMALL BOX
2 quantities Chocolate Gingerbread
gold dusting powder
vegetable oil
115g/4oz plain
(semisweet) chocolate

♥ COOK'S TIP ♥
Once you have assembled both boxes, leave them to set, then line them with tissue paper and fill with chocolates, cookies or sweets (candies). Position the lids and wrap with ribbons. Before allowing anyone to eat your boxes, remove the gold dusting powder decorations as this powder is not edible.

1 Preheat the oven to 180°C/350°F/ Gas 4. Roll out two-thirds of the dough and transfer to a greased baking sheet. Cut out two 18 x 9cm/ 7 x 3½in rectangles for the base and lid of the larger box. Cut two 18 x 5.5cm/7 x 2¼in rectangles for the long sides and two 9 x 5.5cm/3½ x 2¼in rectangles for the short sides.

2 Using a decorative cutter, cut out a row of shapes from all the side sections. Roll out the remaining dough to make the smaller box. Make base and lid sections, 13 x 7.5cm/5 x 3in, the long sides 13 x 5.5cm/5 x 2¼in and the short sides 7.5 x 5.5cm/3 x 2¼in. Decorate the sides. Bake in the oven for 15 minutes. Cool, then trim.

3 Mix the gold dusting powder with a few drops of oil to a good consistency for painting. Paint a pattern around the cut-out edges of the sides. Melt the chocolate. Put a little chocolate in a paper piping bag and snip off the tip.

4 To assemble the large box, pipe a little chocolate along the inside, base edge of one side. Secure it to the base. Secure the remaining three sides, piping more chocolate down the corners. Assemble the smaller box in the same way.

WOODCUTTER'S COTTAGE

Unlike the other 'buildings', this hut is assembled from 'logs' of gingerbread dough, to give it a woody, rustic appearance. For presentation, light a couple of night lights inside the hut, but don't leave them burning long as the gingerbread will char.

2 quantities Chocolate
Gingerbread mixture
1 quantity Lebkuchen mixture
1 quantity royal icing
25cm/10in square cake board
2 flaked chocolate sticks
icing (confectioners') sugar,
for dusting

1 Preheat the oven to 180°C/350°F/ Gas 4. Line a baking sheet. From paper, cut out a 17 x 10cm/6½ x 4in rectangle for the roof, two 15 x 8cm/ 6 x 3¼in rectangles for the hut front and back and two 8 x 7cm/3¼ x 2¾in rectangles for the hut sides.

2 Divide the chocolate dough into 14 pieces. Roll one piece under the palms of your hands to form a rope, 34cm/13½in long. Put it in the centre of the baking sheet. Repeat with the remaining small pieces of dough, spacing them on the baking sheet about 3mm/⅛in apart. Bake for 15 minute. Leave to cool.

3 Lay the roof template over one end of the cooked gingerbread slab and cut it out. Cut out the sides, the front and back sections. Remove from the lining paper. From the front section, cut out a door and window.

4 Put some royal icing in a paper piping bag and snip off the tip. Using a metal spatula, spread the cake board with the remaining royal icing. Pipe a little icing down the side of the front wall and secure to one side wall on the iced board. Secure the other side wall and back in the same way. Cut some lengths of flaked chocolate and reserve for decoration. Crumble the remainder into the hut. Lay the roof section over the hut.

  Make a template of the two trees (see back of book). Roll the Lebkuchen dough and cut out 10 large trees and 15 small trees. Bake on a greased baking sheet for 10 minutes. Leave on the baking sheet for 3 minutes, and then transfer to a wire rack.

5 Pipe a line of icing down one side of a tree section. Secure another straight side of a tree section against the first and place on the board. Add three more parts to make one tree. Construct and position the remaining trees in the same way.

6 Stack the chocolate sticks against one side of the hut as 'logs'. Fit the roof section over the hut. To finish, dust the hut with icing sugar.

♥ COOK'S TIP ♥
Before you begin cutting, lay all the template pieces on the gingerbread, to find the most economical cutting layout.

GILDED GINGERBREAD CROWN

This project requires quite a bit of 'propping up' and leaving to set during the construction, but the results are impressive. Fill the crown with a selection of cookies or chocolate but don't pack them too tightly, or you may weaken the crown.

1 quantity Chocolate
Gingerbread mixture
1 quantity Golden
Gingerbread mixture
2 empty 400g/14oz cans, washed
115g/4oz plain (semisweet) chocolate
1 empty 800g/1lb 12oz can, washed
50g/2oz sugar paste
gold dusting powder
vegetable oil or clear alcohol

1 Preheat the oven to 180°C/350°F/ Gas 4. Roll out two-thirds of the chocolate mixture and cut out eight 12 x 4.5cm/4½ x 1¾ in rectangles. Put on a greased baking sheet. Roll out a little golden gingerbread mixture and cut out eight 4.5 x 2.5cm/1¾ x 1in rectangles. Cut a heart shape from each. Position these rectangles on the chocolate rectangles. Cut two strips of chocolate gingerbread.

2 From the strips, cut out eight triangles that measure 4cm/1½in along the short edge and 5cm/2in from the centre of the short edge to the point. Cover the small cans with foil and support them on the baking sheet. Lay three triangles over each can, so they bake in a curved shape. Bake the gingerbread, allowing about 5 minutes for the small pieces and 15 minutes for the large. Cool on a rack.

3 *(Left)* Melt the chocolate and leave it to cool slightly. Put in a paper piping bag and snip off a small tip. Wrap a band of greaseproof (waxed) paper around the large can and stand it on a reel of adhesive tape or a can that will raise it by about 5cm/2in. Pipe a line of chocolate down one large rectangle and a dot of chocolate on the greaseproof-covered can. Rest the rectangle against the dot of chocolate on the can. Pipe a line of chocolate around another rectangle and secure it to the first. Repeat all the way around, until the rectangles meet. (If they don't fit accurately, you might need to trim one rectangle down slightly.) Leave in a cool place to set. Remove the can and greaseproof paper and transfer the crown to a plate or board. Pipe little dots or scallops of chocolate down the joins in the gingerbread.

4 Pipe a line of chocolate along one rectangle top and secure a gingerbread triangle to it, propping the two up on a jar or carton until the chocolate has set completely. Repeat on the remaining sections; if possible, set a few at a time.

Roll the sugar paste into small balls and make a hole in each with a skewer. Pipe a dot of chocolate on to the tip of each triangle and gently press a sugar paste ball in position. Mix the gold dusting powder to a painting consistency with a few drops of the oil or alcohol. Using the gold paint and a fine paintbrush, paint the balls and the edges of the hearts. Fill the crown with gingerbread cookies and arrange some others around the crown on the plate or board. Store in a cool place.

♥ *COOK'S TIP* ♥
The gold paint is for decoration only and should not be eaten.

DECORATED CHOCOLATE LEBKUCHEN

Wrapped in paper or cellophane, or beautifully boxed, these decorated cookies make a lovely present. Don't make them too far in advance as the chocolate will gradually discolour.

MAKES ABOUT 40
1 quantity Lebkuchen mixture
115g/4oz plain (semisweet) chocolate
115g/4oz milk chocolate
115g/4oz white chocolate
chocolate vermicelli
unsweetened cocoa powder or icing
(confectioners') sugar, for dusting

♥ COOK'S TIP ♥

If the chocolate in the bowls starts to set before you have finished decorating, put the bowls back over the heat for a minute or two. If the chocolate in the piping bags starts to harden, microwave briefly or put in a clean bowl over a pan of simmering water.

1 Grease two baking sheets. Roll out just over half the Lebkuchen mixture to an 8mm/⅜in thickness. Cut out heart shapes, using a 4.5cm/1¾in heart-shaped cutter. Transfer to the baking sheets. Gather the trimmings together with the remaining dough and cut into 20 pieces. Roll into balls and place on the baking sheets. Flatten each one slightly. Chill both sheets for 30 minutes. Preheat the oven to 180°C/350°F/Gas 4. Bake for 8–10 minutes. Cool on a wire rack.

2 Break the plain chocolate into pieces and melt in a heatproof bowl over a small pan of gently simmering water. Melt the milk and white chocolate in separate bowls. Spoon a little of each chocolate into three paper piping bags and reserve. Spoon a little plain chocolate over a third of the cookies, spreading it slightly to cover them completely. (Tapping the rack gently will help the chocolate to run down the sides.)

3 Snip the merest tip from the bag of white chocolate and drizzle it over some of the coated cookies.

4 Scatter the chocolate vermicelli over the plain chocolate cookies that haven't been decorated. Coat the remaining cookies with the milk and white chocolate and decorate some of these with more chocolate from the piping bags, contrasting the colours. Scatter more undecorated cookies with vermicelli. Leave to set.

5 Transfer the undecorated cookies to a plate or tray and dust lightly with cocoa powder or icing sugar.

CRENELLATED CASTLE

*T**his impressive castle would make a lovely birthday cake for any young child. If liked, you could add some chocolate soldiers or small, non-edible decorations. Bake the dough pieces in batches if necessary, and make sure that they are cooled on a flat surface.*

1 quantity Lebkuchen mixture
2 quantities Golden
Gingerbread mixture
200g/7oz plain (semisweet) chocolate
115g/4oz milk chocolate
35cm/14in square cake board
or tray

1 Preheat the oven to 180°C/350°F/ Gas 4. Grease two baking sheets. Make one template (see back of book) of the castle back wall, one of the left side wall, three of the front, two of the keep ends, two of the front sides and one of the entrance. From paper, cut out two 14 x 12cm/ 5½ x 4½in rectangles for the castle keep sides, two 13 x 6cm/5 x 2½in rectangles for the keep roof and one 11 x 5cm/ 4½ x 2in rectangle for the drawbridge.

2 Roll out the Lebkuchen mixture to a 26cm/10½in square and transfer to a baking sheet. Bake for 20 minutes, then cool. Roll out half the golden gingerbread. Lay some templates on the dough and cut around. Transfer to a baking sheet. Roll out the remaining dough, and cut out the other shapes.

3 Bake the dough for 15 minutes, until it begins to turn golden around the edges. Leave on the baking sheets for 3 minutes and then transfer to a wire rack to cool. For the portcullis, draw two 5cm/2in squares on greaseproof (waxed) paper. Melt the plain and milk chocolate in separate heatproof bowls over pans of barely simmering water. Put the melted chocolate in paper piping bags and snip off the ends. Pipe lines of the plain chocolate 3mm/⅛in apart on the squares. Pipe more lines in the opposite direction. Pipe four thick lines, 9cm/3½in long on to the paper for the drawbridge 'chains'. Leave in a cool place to set. (One trellis and two of the chocolate strips are 'spares', in case of breakage!)

4 Pipe a line of melted plain chocolate around the entrance arch. Pipe another line about 1cm/½in from the crenellated top. Using the melted milk chocolate, pipe a decorative design around the arch. Pipe an outline around the top edge of the gingerbread.

♥ *COOK'S TIP* ♥
Let the chocolate cool slightly before using it to 'glue' the castle sections together, otherwise the sections will not adhere. When securing the portcullis, use cool hands and work fairly quickly. Long, thin chocolate mints can be used instead of piped chocolate strips to create the drawbridge.

▶

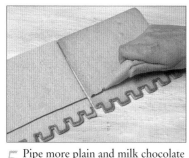

5 Pipe more plain and milk chocolate on to the other wall sections of the castle, lining up the walls so that the dark chocolate piping lines up. Leave all the pieces to set.

6 Carefully slide the Lebkuchen base on to a cake board or tray. Pipe a line of plain chocolate along the base of the entrance section. Place on the gingerbread base, about 5cm/2in from the front edge. Prop the section against a can for support.

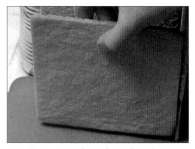

7 Pipe more plain chocolate down one entrance side section and secure carefully in place, supporting as before. Secure the other entrance side section, and then the front sections, in the same way. Strengthen by piping more chocolate down the joins and along the base on the inside. Leave the chocolate to set.

8 Carefully peel the paper from the piped chocolate square. Handling the chocolate as little as possible, pipe a little chocolate around the edges and then secure to the wrong side of the arch, to resemble a portcullis. Secure the remaining front section to the right side of the castle, at right angles to the front. Pipe a little chocolate along the exposed edge and then carefully rest one keep end section against it.

9 Pipe chocolate along the short sides of the keep side sections and stick them in place. Fix the remaining wall sections of the castle in position, propping them up while they set, where necessary. Leave the chocolate to set. Secure the drawbridge in place with chocolate. Position the chocolate strips from the entrance walls to the drawbridge as the 'chains', securing with a little chocolate.

10 Pipe more chocolate along the roof edges of the keep and then secure the roof pieces in position. Finally, use more chocolate to pipe small, cross-shaped windows over the castle walls and on the keep. Leave to set in a cool place.

STEAM TRAIN

For presentation, set this magnificent train on a 33cm/13in square cake board, which you have covered with a thin layer of grey or black sugar paste. Any gingerbread trimmings can be shaped into a simple track for the train.

3 quantities Chocolate
Gingerbread mixture
2 empty 400g/14oz cans, washed
175g/6oz plain (semisweet) chocolate
15cm/6in square sponge cake
icing (confectioners') sugar,
for dusting
115g/4oz green sugar paste
115g/4oz black sugar paste

1 Preheat the oven to 180°C/350°F/ Gas 4. Grease three large baking sheets. From paper, cut out a 30 x 13cm/12 x 5in rectangle for the train base, a 13 x 1cm/5 x ½in rectangle for the bumper section, two 20 x 5cm/ 8 x 2in rectangles for the long sides and a 13 x 7cm/5 x 2¾in rectangle for the cab roof.

2 Roll out half the gingerbread dough and cut around the templates. Transfer to one baking sheet. Cover each can with foil and support the cans on the second baking sheet, wedging them with a little dough. Roll out more gingerbread and cut out two 10cm/4in squares. Curve the squares over the cans. Make templates for the cab front and sides and the train front, from the back of the book. Cut around the templates and transfer to the second baking sheet.

3 Cut out a gingerbread man, using a 10cm/4in cutter, and transfer it to the third baking sheet. Halve a cocktail stick (toothpick) and secure a small dough rectangle to one end, for a flag. Lift one of the gingerbread man's arms and press the stick into it. Strengthen by gently pressing another gingerbread ball at the end of the arm.

♥ *COOK'S TIP* ♥
*If you have any
gingerbread mixture left
over, re-roll it and cut out another
gingerbread man to serve as a
stationmaster or guard. You could
even make an extra batch of
dough so that you can shape a
selection of gingerbread
'passengers'. This is ideal for
occupying younger members of the
family while you get on with
the more difficult modelling.*

4 To make the wheels, cut out eight 4cm/1½in rounds, using a pastry cutter. Transfer to the third baking sheet. Cut out the centres of the wheels using a slightly smaller cutter. Cut out two 3cm/1¼in wheels and remove the centres of these. Re-roll the trimmings and cut out long, thin strips. Use to make the wheel spokes, cutting them to fit. Bake all the gingerbread, in batches if necessary, allowing about 8–10 minutes for the wheels and 15 minutes for the larger sections. Leave on the baking sheets for 3 minutes and then transfer to a wire rack to cool. (Stand the curved sections on one end to cool, so they don't collapse.) Trim the edges straight, if necessary.

▶

5 Melt half the chocolate and leave it to cool slightly. Put some in a paper piping bag and snip off the tip. Spread a little chocolate along one long side of a side section and secure this to the train base about 2cm/¾in in from the side and front of the train. Prop up the side with a jar until the chocolate has hardened. Position the other side section in the same way.

6 Spread more chocolate around the edges of the train front and stick it in position. Leave to set for 10 minutes. Spread melted chocolate around the edges of one curved section and gently rest it over the side sections. Position the second curved section. Use more chocolate to secure the train cab, first sticking the front in position and then the sides and finally the roof. Leave for 10 minutes.

7 Halve the sponge cake and lay the halves end to end on a board or tray, to make a raised base, cutting off one end so that it is about 25cm/10in long. Using a fish slice or metal spatula, carefully lift the train and place it on the sponge cake. Use more chocolate to secure the bumper section to the front, propping it on a box or crumpled foil until set.

8 Thinly roll a little green sugar paste on a surface dusted with icing sugar and cut out long thin strips. Cut into short lengths and use to decorate the wheel spokes, securing with a dot of chocolate. Press a small ball of black sugar paste into the centre of each. Secure the wheels to the sides of the cake with a little melted chocolate.

9 Melt the remaining chocolate and put it in a paper piping bag. Snip off a small tip. Use the chocolate to pipe little dots or scallops around the joins in the gingerbread. Pipe two further rows of chocolate over the centre of each curved section.

10 Thinly roll a little green sugar paste and cut into 4cm/1½in lengths. Secure in loops along the sides of the train. Use more green and black sugar paste to shape the remaining decorations, securing them with melted chocolate. Decorate the gingerbread men with sugar paste and secure him to the cab. Leave in a cool place to set.

GINGERBREAD TEDDIES

These endearing teddies, dressed in striped pyjamas, would make a perfect gift for friends of any age. If you can't get a large cutter, make smaller teddies or use a traditional gingerbread-man cutter. Just adding little semi-circles of dough for ears instantly makes them teddy-like!

MAKES 6
1 quantity Golden
Gingerbread mixture
75g/3oz white chocolate
175g/6oz white sugar paste
icing (confectioners') sugar,
for dusting
blue food colouring
25g/1oz plain (semisweet) or
milk chocolate

1 Preheat the oven to 180°C/350°F/ Gas 4. Grease two large baking sheets. Roll out the gingerbread dough on a floured surface and cut out gingerbread teddies, using a 13cm/5in teddy cookie cutter. Transfer to the baking sheets and bake for 10–15 minutes, until they are just beginning to colour around the edges. Leave on the baking sheets for 3 minutes and then transfer to a wire rack to cool.

2 Melt half the white chocolate. Put in a paper piping bag and snip off the tip. Make a neat template for the teddies' clothes: draw an outline of the cutter on to paper, finishing at the neck, halfway down the arms and around the legs. Thinly roll the sugar paste on a surface dusted with icing sugar. Use the template to cut out the clothes, and secure them to the teddies with the chocolate. Use the sugar paste trimmings to add ears, eyes and snouts.

3 Dilute the blue colouring with a little water and use it to paint the striped pyjamas, leaving a little white collar and painting in a waistline.

4 *(Left)* Gently melt the remaining white chocolate and the plain or milk chocolate in separate bowls over pans of barely simmering water. Put in separate paper piping bags and snip off the tips. Use the white chocolate to pipe a decorative outline around the pyjamas and use the plain or milk chocolate to pipe the faces.

JEWELLED ELEPHANTS

These stunningly robed elephants make a lovely gift for animal-lovers, or an edible decoration for a special occasion. If you make holes in them for hanging before baking, you could hang them as stunningly original Christmas tree decorations.

MAKES ABOUT 10
1 quantity Lebkuchen mixture
1 quantity Royal Icing
red food colouring
225g/8oz sugar paste
small candy-covered chocolates
or chews
gold dragees

1 Preheat the oven to 180°C/350°F/ Gas 4. Grease two large baking sheets. Make a paper template for the elephant by enlarging the one at the back of the book by 25 per cent. Roll out the Lebkuchen mixture. Use the template and a sharp knife to cut out elephant shapes. Space them, slightly apart, on the baking sheets. Re-roll the trimmings to make more elephants. Bake for 12 minutes, until they are just turning golden. Leave on the baking sheet for 3 minutes and then transfer to a wire rack to cool.

3 Roll out the white sugar paste. Cut out circles, using a 6cm/2½in cookie cutter. Secure to the elephants' backs with royal icing so that the edge of the sugar paste is about 2.5cm/1in above the top of the legs. Trim off the excess paste around the top of the white sugar paste shapes.

2 Put a little royal icing in a paper piping bag and then cut off the tip of the bag. Knead some red food colouring into half the sugar paste. Roll a little red sugar paste under your fingers to create fine ropes. Secure these ropes around the feet and tips of the trunks, using icing from the bag. Shape more red sugar paste into flat oval shapes, about 2cm/¾in long, and stick them to the elephants' heads in the same way. Shape smaller ovals and secure them at the top of the trunks.

4 *(Left)* Pipe 1cm/½in tassels around the edges. Pipe dots of white icing at the tops of the trunks, around the necks and at the tops of the tails and also use it to draw small eyes. Halve the small sweets (candies) and press into the sugar paste, above the tassels. Decorate the headdresses, sweets and white sugar paste with dragees, securing them with dots of icing. Leave for several hours, to harden.

DOUBLE GINGERBREAD COOKIES

*Packed in little bags or into a gingerbread box, these pretty cookies would make a lovely gift.
They are easy to make, but will have everyone wondering how you did it!*

MAKES ABOUT 25
1 quantity Chocolate
Gingerbread mixture
1 quantity Golden
Gingerbread mixture

1 Roll out half the chocolate dough on a floured surface to a 28 x 4cm/ 11 x 1¼in rectangle, 1cm/½in thick. Repeat with half the golden gingerbread dough. Using a knife, cut both lengths into seven long, thin strips. Lay the strips together, side by side, alternating the colours.

2 Roll out the remaining golden gingerbread dough with your hands to a long sausage, 2cm/¾in wide and the length of the strips. Lay the sausage of dough down the centre of the striped dough. Carefully bring the striped dough up around the sausage and press it gently in position, to enclose the sausage completely. Roll the remaining chocolate dough to a thin rectangle measuring 28 x 13cm/ 11 x 5in.

3 Bring the chocolate dough up around the striped dough, to enclose it. Press gently into place. Wrap and chill for 30 minutes.

4 Preheat the oven to 180°C/350°F/ Gas 4. Grease a large baking sheet. Cut the gingerbread roll into thin slices and place them, slightly apart, on the prepared baking sheet. Bake for about 12–15 minutes, until just beginning to colour around the edges. Leave to cool on the baking sheet for 3 minutes and then transfer to a wire rack to cool completely.

♥ COOK'S TIP ♥

For slicing the cookie dough before baking, use a knife that will cut cleanly through: a serrated kitchen knife usually works well. For a fresh supply of the cookies, bake them in batches; the shaped dough will store well in the refrigerator for up to a week, or it freezes well.

FRUIT-LADEN GINGERBREAD

Many gingerbread recipes have a more spongy, cake-like texture than the gingerbread cookies used for constructions, and they can be flavoured with dried fruit, nuts and a variety of delicious spices. This version contains plenty of raisins, ginger pieces and orange, and is decorated with fruits, perfect for a treat with fresh, strong coffee.

Serves 16
450g/1lb/4 cups plain
(all-purpose) flour
5ml/1 tsp baking powder
15ml/1 tbsp ground ginger
5ml/1 tsp ground cinnamon
225g/8oz/1½ cups raisins
75g/3oz/½ cup blanched almonds,
roughly chopped
50g/2oz/¼ cup glacé (candied) cherries
finely grated rind of 1 orange
100g/3½oz/½ cup chopped glacé
(candied) or crystallized ginger
225g/8oz/1 cup unsalted butter
225g/8oz/⅔ cup golden
(light corn) syrup
150g/5oz/¾ cup dark muscovado
(molasses) sugar
4 eggs, beaten
1 quantity Icing Glaze
450g/1lb mixed glacé fruits

1 Preheat the oven to 190°C/375°F/ Gas 5. Grease and line a 20cm/8in square cake tin (pan). Sift the flour, baking powder, ginger and cinnamon into a bowl. Stir in the raisins and almonds. Halve the cherries, then add with the orange rind and half the crystallized ginger. Heat the butter, syrup and sugar in a pan until the butter has melted. Add to the bowl, with the eggs, and mix to combine.

2 Tip the gingerbread mixture into the tin and bake for 15 minutes. Reduce the oven temperature to 160°C/325°F/ Gas 3 and bake for a further hour, or until the gingerbread is firm to the touch and a skewer, inserted into the centre, comes out clean. Leave to cool in the tin.

♥ *COOK'S TIP* ♥
This cake keeps well. Wrap and store in an airtight container before decorating it, adding the icing and fruit the day before you are going to serve it.

3 Remove from the tin. Spread half the icing glaze over the top. Arrange the fruits and ginger over the glaze.

4 Drizzle the fruits with the rest of the glaze and leave for several hours, until the glaze has set. Tie a ribbon around the cake, if you like, and serve cut in squares.

NOAH'S ARK

This impressive creation is good fun to make and would undoubtedly give a lot of pleasure to a young child for a birthday celebration. Several animal templates are provided (see back of book) but you may already have plenty of animal cutters. If not, animal cutters are also widely available in kitchenware and gift stores.

3 quantities Golden
Gingerbread mixture
200g/7oz white chocolate
225g/8oz blue sugar paste
icing (confectioners') sugar,
for dusting
115g/4oz green sugar paste
33cm/13in round silver cake board

1 Preheat the oven to 180°C/350°F/ Gas 4. Line two large baking sheets with baking parchment. Make templates of the ark sides, cabin ends and the animals, if using (see back of book). From paper, cut out a 27 x 8cm/ 10¾ x 3¼in rectangle for the deck, a 21 x 4cm/8¼ x 1½in rectangle for the ramp, two 14 x 8cm/5½ x 3¼in rectangles for the ark ends, two 10 x 4cm/4 x 1½in rectangles for the cabin sides and two 12 x 6cm/4½ x 2½in rectangles for the roof. Lay the ark sides template under the baking parchment on one baking sheet.

2 Roll out half the gingerbread dough on a floured surface. Cut out long strips, 2cm/¾in wide. Lay one strip across the top of the template, so the edge of the dough is level with the edge of the template. Lay another strip so that it slightly overlaps the first. Repeat until the template is covered and then trim off the sloping ends. Slide the template from under the paper and make another side in the same way. Cut a 5cm/2in notch from the top edge of one side section, for supporting the ramp. Place the roof templates under the paper and lay strips on it in the same way. Roll out more dough and cut out all the remaining template shapes in the same way. Transfer to baking sheets and bake, allowing about 10 minutes for the smaller shapes and 20–25 minutes for the ark sides. Leave on the baking sheets for 3 minutes, then cool on a wire rack.

3 Melt half the chocolate in a bowl resting over a pan of barely boiling water and leave it to cool slightly. Put the chocolate in a paper piping bag and snip off the end. Pipe the melted chocolate down the long side of one ark end and position it along the sloping side of one ark side. Prop them up with some sort of container so the side is supported at an angle of 90°. Leave to set. ▶

♥ COOK'S TIP ♥
For the best result, bake the gingerbread animals facing in the direction you want them to be on the finished cake (the underside will not be so smooth and attractive). Flip some of them over, still in pairs, before baking, if you want to have them facing different directions.

4 Secure the other ark end in place, supporting it as before. Gently rest the other ark side on the ends. Make sure the ark will sit squarely, once upright, by resting a flat tray against the ark base: all pieces should be level. Leave the chocolate in a cool place to set.

5 Carefully turn the ark upright. Pipe more chocolate inside the ark, along the joins, to reinforce them. Leave in a cool place to set. Assemble the cabin by piping chocolate down the sides of the pieces and sticking them together. Leave to set.

6 Pipe more chocolate along the edges of the roof sections and then carefully rest the roof in place. Pipe a little chocolate around the deck and lay it in position. Rest the cabin on top and leave to set in a cool place.

7 Thinly roll out the blue sugar paste on a surface dusted with icing sugar. Lightly brush the cake board with water. Lift the sugar paste on to the board to cover two-thirds of it. Roll out the green sugar paste and use it to cover the remaining board, so it overlaps the blue sugar paste by about 4cm/1½in. Using a knife, cut a wavy line through the overlapping thicknesses of icing. Lift out the excess blue and green paste and smooth down the pastes so they meet in a neat, wavy line.

8 Carefully lift the ark on to the blue paste, towards the back of the board, so that, when the ramp is positioned, it reaches the green paste. Melt the remaining white chocolate in a bowl resting over a pan of simmering water. Put the melted chocolate in a paper piping bag. Snip off a small tip. Use this melted chocolate to pipe little dots or decorative scallops around the joins of the ark. This acts as a decorative edging at the same time as giving additional strength to all the joints.

9 Use more melted chocolate to thinly pipe features on to the animals, that is, eyes, mouths, tails and so on. You can also try outlining other bits of their bodies to give the animals more definition. Stick the animals in pairs by sandwiching them, about 2cm/¾in apart, with a little left-over icing. Arrange the animals on the ark and the 'land' in whatever way pleases you. The good thing about the free-standing pairs of animals is that you can fiddle about until you are entirely happy with the result.

HANSEL AND GRETEL COTTAGE

L avishly decorated with an assortment of colourful confections, this gingerbread house is great fun to assemble. If you make it as a birthday cake, you will find that picking off the various treats is far more exciting than eating a traditional sponge-based party cake.

*2 quantities Golden
Gingerbread mixture
1 quantity Royal Icing
white chocolate buttons
coloured boiled sweets (candies)
large selection of small sweets
and jellies*

♥ *COOK'S TIP* ♥
*The whole family can enjoy
decorating this cake as 'anything
goes'! It can also be reused
at Christmas with plenty of
candy canes and a light dusting
of icing (confectioners') sugar.*

1 Preheat the oven to 180°C/350°F/
Gas 4. Grease two large baking
sheets. From paper, cut out two
16 x 7cm/6¼ x 2¾in rectangles for the
cottage roof and two 15 x 14cm/6 x
5½in rectangles for the front and back.
For the sides, shape two 14 x 7.5cm/
5½ x 3in rectangles, adding a pointed
roof section to one short side that
measures 2.5cm/1¾in from the tip of
the point to the edge of the rectangle.

3 Bake all the gingerbread, allowing
5 minutes for the small pieces and
about 15 minutes for the large pieces,
or until just beginning to colour
around the edges. Leave on the
baking sheets for 3 minutes and then
transfer to a wire rack to cool. Trim
the pieces, if necessary.

2 Roll out half the gingerbread.
Cut out twelve 5 x 2.5cm/2 x 1in
rectangles of gingerbread and cut
notches on one long side of each for
'curtains'. Using the templates, cut
out the house sections. Cut out
windows from the front and side
sections and mark a small door with
a knife. Mark vertical lines on the
door and cut out a small heart shape.
Re-roll the gingerbread trimmings
and cut out a 23cm/9in round.

4 Put some royal icing in a paper piping bag and cut off the tip. Pipe a little icing down the long sides of the curtain sections and secure them to the insides of the windows, so the curtains show through.

5 Pipe a little royal icing down one short side of the front section and stick it at right angles to a side section, on the gingerbread base. Pipe more icing inside the house along the base, to hold it firmly. Use a can or jar to prop the walls in position while the icing sets (in a cool place).

6 Stick the other side section and back of the house in position. Pipe more icing along the top edges of the gingerbread and position the roof pieces. Leave to set in a cool place.

7 Pipe a wavy line of icing along the bottom edge of the roof and stick on a row of chocolate buttons. Pipe a line of icing above the buttons and stick on a row of boiled sweets. Repeat the layering, to cover the roof.

8 Pipe another line of icing along the top of the roof and secure a row of halved chocolate buttons. Pipe dots of icing along the inner edges of the cottage curtains.

9 Use lots of sweets to decorate the cottage, sticking them in place with plenty of royal icing. To make the front path, stick on pieces of broken chocolate buttons. Pipe simple flower outlines on to the walls and in the garden area and press small sweets into the centres.

SWEET NECKLACES

These novelty necklaces are made from tiny gingerbread cookies, decorated and threaded on to ribbons. Arrange in a pretty, tissue-lined box or tin for presentation.

MAKES 12 NECKLACES
1 quantity Lebkuchen mixture
1 quantity Royal Icing
pink food colouring
selection of small sweets (candies)
6m/6 yards fine pink, blue or white ribbon

♥ *COOK'S TIP* ♥
Use liquorice bootlaces instead of lengths of ribbon for threading the cookies to make totally edible necklaces, perfect for presenting as party gifts.

1 Preheat the oven to 180°C/350°F/ Gas 4. Grease two large baking sheets. Roll out slightly more than half the gingerbread mixture on a lightly floured surface to a thickness of 5mm/¼in. Cut out stars using a 2.5cm/1in star cutter. Transfer the stars to a baking sheet and spread them out evenly. Taking care not to distort the shape of the stars, make a large hole in the centre of each one, using a metal or wooden skewer.

2 Gather the trimmings together with the remaining dough. Roll the dough under the palms of your hands, to make a thick sausage about 2.5cm/1in in diameter. Cut in 1cm/½in slices. Using the skewer, make a hole in the centre of each. Put on the second baking sheet. Bake the gingerbread for about 8 minutes, until slightly risen and just beginning to colour. Remove from the oven and, while still warm, re-make the skewer holes as the gingerbread will have spread slightly during baking. Transfer to a wire rack to cool.

3 Put half the royal icing in a paper piping bag and snip off a small tip. Use to pipe outlines around the star cookies. Colour the remaining icing pale pink. Put it in a paper piping bag fitted with a star nozzle. Pipe stars on to the round cookies. Cut the sweets into smaller pieces and use to decorate the cookies. Leave to harden.

4 *(Left)* Cut the ribbon into 50cm/ 20in lengths. Thread a selection of the cookies on to each ribbon.

MARQUETRY HEARTS

M arquetry is the decorative technique of inlaying contrastingly-coloured woods. Although very simple to do, fitting light and dark gingerbread shapes together to create a pattern or picture is very effective. Use this idea as inspiration for creating your own marquetry-style plaques.

*1 quantity Chocolate
Gingerbread mixture
1 quantity Golden
Gingerbread mixture*

1 Preheat the oven to 180°C/350°F/ Gas 4. Roll out the chocolate and gingerbread mixtures 5mm/¼in thick. Cut out 12 4.5cm/1¾in squares from the chocolate gingerbread and 13 4.5cm/1¾in squares from the golden gingerbread. Assemble the squares in a checkerboard design on a lined baking sheet with golden squares in the corners.

2 Using a 4cm/1½in heart-shaped cutter, neatly cut out a heart shape from each one of the golden gingerbread squares.

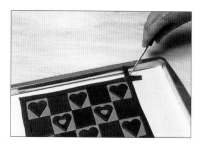

3 Using the same cutter, cut out 13 hearts from the remaining chocolate gingerbread and press them into the golden squares with heart-shaped holes. Using a 1.5cm/⅝in heart-shaped cutter, cut out heart shapes from the four chocolate squares illustrated and position a golden gingerbread heart of the same size in the spaces.

4 (*Left*) Re-roll all the gingerbread trimmings and cut four long, thin strips from each. Position a chocolate strip down each side of the cookie, overlapping them at the corners. Using a knife, mitre the corners by cutting through both thicknesses and removing the dough ends. Position the strips of golden gingerbread mixture outside the chocolate border and trim the corners, as before. Bake for about 15 minutes. Leave on the baking sheet to cool.

ROCKING-HORSE COOKIES

*B*rightly decorated with red and blue sugar paste, these simple rocking-horses are really absorbing to make. Make them for gifts and pack them into pretty, tissue-lined boxes.

MAKES 6–8
1 quantity Lebkuchen mixture
1 quantity Royal Icing
50g/2oz red sugar paste
icing (confectioners') sugar, for dusting
50g/2oz blue sugar paste
50g/2oz black sugar paste

♥ *COOK'S TIP* ♥
Re-roll the gingerbread trimmings for the rockers. Cut straight strips and bend them gently into curves on the baking sheets, making sure they are securely fixed to the horses' feet.

1 Preheat the oven to 180°C/350°F/ Gas 4. Grease two large baking sheets. Make a rocking-horse template (see back of book). Roll out the gingerbread on a floured surface and cut out the shapes. Space them well apart on the baking sheets. Cut out 15cm/6in long strips, about 1cm/½in wide, to make the rockers. Bake the gingerbread for about 10 minutes, until slightly risen and just beginning to colour. Leave on the baking sheets for 3 minutes and then transfer to a wire rack.

2 Put a little royal icing in a paper piping bag, fitted with a small writing nozzle. Roll out the red sugar paste on a surface dusted with icing sugar. Cut out saddles, using the template as a guide, and stick one to each horse with a little royal icing. Thinly roll the blue sugar paste and cut it into long thin strips. Secure these to the horses with a little icing, to form the reins and bridles.

3 Roll out the black sugar paste and cut out manes and tails, using the template. Stick them to the cookies in the same way.

4 Put more icing in the piping bag to pipe eyes and decorative designs on the saddles and rockers. Leave for several hours in a cool place, to set.

GINGERBREAD STREET

*I*ndulge your creativity with these pretty gingerbread houses, simply decorated with piped chocolate and glazed 'windows'. Copy the design used here or make your own street scene in the design and size of your choice.

MAKES 6–8
1 quantity Golden
Gingerbread mixture
115g/4oz boiled sweets (hard candies)
50g/2oz plain (semisweet) or
milk chocolate
several thin sticks of chocolate

♥ *COOK'S TIP* ♥

If cutting out 'door' sections, remember to leave a thin frame of gingerbread at the bottom, so that the sweets (candies) don't run out as they melt, making an uneven edge.

1 Preheat the oven to 180°C/350°F/ Gas 4. Line two baking sheets with non-stick baking parchment. Draw a 17 x 8cm/6½ x 3¼in rectangle on a sheet of paper. Draw several roof outlines along one long edge and fill the rectangle with a variety of windows. Cut out the template.

2 Roll out the gingerbread dough on a floured surface, lay the template on top and cut around the template outline. Transfer to the baking sheet and then remove the window sections. Bake for 5 minutes.

3 Lightly crush the boiled sweets by tapping them firmly, still in their wrappers, with the end of a rolling pin. Put the sweets into the window areas of the gingerbread and bake for a further 5 minutes, until the sweets melt to fill the windows. Cool on the baking sheets.

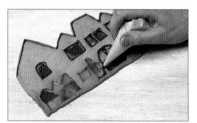

4 Melt the chocolate and leave it to cool slightly. Put it into a paper piping bag and snip off the tip. Use the chocolate to pipe roof, window and door outlines on the houses.

5 Pipe lines of chocolate under the windows and stick the chocolate sticks in place, cutting them to fit where necessary. Leave in a cool place until the chocolate has set.

HARVEST PLAQUE

*Decorated with simple fruits and flowers, this large cookie makes a delicious autumnal gift.
Loosely wrap it in tissue paper and pack it in a flat box or tin.*

2 quantities Golden
Gingerbread mixture
50g/2oz white almond paste
several whole cloves, buds removed
½ quantity Royal Icing
orange, green and yellow
food colourings

1 Preheat the oven to 180°C/350°F/ Gas 4. Grease a baking sheet. Roll out two-thirds of the gingerbread dough and cut out a 22 x 18cm/8½ x 7in rectangle. Transfer to the prepared baking sheet. Using the handle end of a fine paintbrush, make small decorative indentations around the edges. With the tip of a knife, mark a line 1.5cm/⅝in away from all the edges. Lightly grease a sectioned tartlet tin (pan). Thinly roll the remaining dough and cut out simple flower shapes, using appropriate cookie cutters.

2 Press the shapes against the sides of the tartlet tin, so that they bake in a cupped position. Roll small balls from the trimmings and press them into the centres. Re-roll the trimmings and cut out simple leaves, each about 5cm/2in long and 2.5cm/1in wide. Arrange the leaves in the tin with the flowers, with some curving into the tartlet cases so they bake in a curved shape. Bake the gingerbread base for about 20 minutes and the flowers and leaves for about 7 minutes. Leave to cool in the tin.

3 Lightly knead the almond paste and divide it in half. Roll each half into a ball and roll the balls over a fine grater, to give a textured surface. Slice them in half and press a clove into each half to form the fruits.

4 (*Left*) Put a little of the icing in a paper piping bag and snip off the tip. Use to secure the flowers, fruit and leaves to the gingerbread plaque. (You might prefer to try a few different arrangements of decorations first, before you stick them in place.) Dilute the orange food colouring with a little water and use it to paint the almond-paste fruits, using a fine paintbrush.

5 Colour half the remaining icing green and thin it with a little water, if necessary, to give a painting consistency. Use to paint decorative lines over the leaves. Colour the remaining icing yellow and use it to paint the centres of the flowers and a decorative line around the edges of the plaque. Leave overnight in a cool place to set.

FESTIVE WREATH

Use this elaborate wreath as a table centrepiece over the festive season: the warm scent of gingerbread and spices will gradually fill the room. To bake the leaves in curved shapes, collect two or three cardboard tubes from the centres of foil or wrapping paper and cover them with foil before draping gingerbread leaves over them.

2 quantities Chocolate
Gingerbread mixture
1 quantity Golden
Gingerbread mixture
8 cinnamon sticks
2m/2 yards ribbon, about
1cm/¹/₂in wide
8–10 kumquats
cloves
50g/2oz red sugar paste
1 quantity Royal Icing
lemon juice
35cm/14in round gold cake
board (optional)

♥ COOK'S TIP ♥
If you can find one, you could use a large holly cutter for shaping the leaves, although the points on cutters are often quite rounded, which doesn't look as effective.

1 Preheat the oven to 180°C/350°F/ Gas 4. Grease two large baking sheets. Roll out two-thirds of the chocolate gingerbread dough on a floured surface until it is about 30cm/12in in diameter. Transfer to one baking sheet. Using a large plate or bowl as a guide, cut out a circle, about 28cm/11in in diameter. Cut an 18cm/7in circle out of the centre and lift out the dough in the centre, to leave a ring of gingerbread.

2 Re-roll the trimmings with the remaining chocolate dough. Cut out oval shapes, about 8cm/3¹/₄in long and 5cm/2in wide. Using a small round cutter or the wide end of a large piping nozzle, cut out flutes from the edges of the oval, to shape large holly leaves. Mark veins on the leaves with a sharp knife.

3 (*Left*) Put the foil-wrapped tubes on a baking sheet, supporting them around the base with a little dough. Lay some leaves over the tubes. Make more leaves from the golden gingerbread, positioning some on the curved tubes and others flat on the baking sheets. You will need about 40. Bake the gingerbread for about 8–10 minutes, until the golden gingerbread is just starting to colour around the edges. Leave on the baking sheets for 3 minutes and then transfer to a wire rack to cool.

4 Tie pairs of cinnamon sticks with short lengths of ribbon. Stud the kumquats with plenty of cloves. Shape the red sugar paste into small 'holly berries'.

5 Put some royal icing in a paper piping bag and snip off the tip, so the icing can be piped in a thick line. Pipe a line of icing around a leaf. Using a paintbrush dipped in lemon juice, draw the icing from the centre of the piped line towards the centre of the leaf, to give a variegated look. Repeat on about a third of the leaves.

6 Carefully slide the gingerbread ring on to the cake board, if using. Pipe a dot of icing on to the tip of a leaf and stick it to the ring. Continue adding more leaves, gradually building up the design with the leaves arranged in different directions.

7 When the leaves are arranged, position the kumquats and cinnamon bundles, securing them with a little icing. Arrange the red berries in clusters among the leaves and finish with additional ribbon if you like.

GOLDEN CHRISTMAS TREE

You can decorate this stunning tree with any combination of confections, chocolate and gingerbread shapes, provided they are not too heavy. It can be used for a really impressive table centrepiece, trimmed with plenty of gold, or a brighter colour scheme.

*3 quantities Golden
Gingerbread mixture
1 quantity Royal Icing
gold dragees
28cm/11in round gold cake board
1 empty 400g/14oz can, washed
selection of gold-wrapped sweets
(candies) or chocolates
1.5m/1½ yards fine gold beading
1.5m/1½ yards fine gold ribbon*

1 Preheat the oven to 180°C/350°F/ Gas 4. Grease two large baking sheets. Thinly roll out one-third of the dough on a floured surface and transfer to one baking sheet. Cut out a 33 x 23cm/13 x 9in rectangle from the dough on the baking sheet; remove the trimmings. Cut the rectangle accurately in half lengthways. Using a long ruler, or two pieces of paper overlapping in a straight line as a guide, cut diagonally from one corner of a rectangle to the other. Repeat on the second rectangle.

♥ *COOK'S TIP* ♥
Make sure the gingerbread shapes cool on a perfectly flat wire rack, as they must be straight to allow you to assemble the tree correctly.

2 Roll just under half the remaining dough, put it on the other baking sheet and cut it in the same way to make four more triangles, as above. Re-roll all the trimmings with the remaining dough and cut out a large selection of stars, boots and other suitable decorative shapes. (Make some large stars, so you can secure one to the top of the tree.) Using a knife, cut out candy cane shapes. Add to the baking sheets and cook, allowing about 8 minutes for the small shapes and 15–20 minutes for the triangles.

3 Immediately the gingerbread is removed from the oven, re-cut the diagonal lines, as the mixture will have risen slightly. Leave on the baking sheets for 3 minutes and then transfer to a wire rack to cool.

4 Trim the straight sides of the triangles using a serrated knife. Put a third of the icing in a piping bag, fitted with a writing nozzle. Pipe dots of icing over one triangle and secure gold dragees to the dots. Repeat on the remaining triangles.

5 Put half the remaining icing in a piping bag fitted with a star nozzle. Pipe a line of icing down the straight side of one triangle and along the base. Repeat on another triangle. ▶

6 Secure the straight sides of the triangles together on the cake board, so they meet at right angles in the centre of the board. Gently rest the empty can over the top of the triangles, to hold them together.

7 Gradually add the remaining triangles to the tree: first position two so that there are four sections at right angles, each time carefully lifting off the can while positioning. Add the remaining four sections in the same way. Leave in a cool place for several hours to set. Lift away the can.

8 Use more icing in the star nozzle to pipe rows of stars over the joins between the tree sections. Decorate the un-iced sides of each section with more gold dragees, using tweezers if that makes it easier to reach the innermost areas.

9 Using the writing nozzle, decorate the little cookies, either by simply piping an icing outline, or by adding additional features. Leave to set.

10 Stick the cookies to the tree by piping a little icing on to the edge of the gingerbread and then gently pressing them into place. Stick a large star to the top of the tree. Stick gold-wrapped sweets between the cookies.

11 Put a dot of icing at the top of the tree behind the star, and secure the end of the gold beading. Loosely trail it around the tree, securing in places with a dot of icing. Repeat with the ribbon. Leave to set.

STAINED-GLASS WINDOWS

*A*lthough they are very easy to make, these cookies look stunning displayed near a window or on the Christmas tree, where they will catch the glow of the Christmas lights.

MAKES ABOUT 10
1 quantity Golden or Chocolate
Gingerbread mixture
about 20 boiled sweets
(hard candies)
fine ribbon or string

♥ COOK'S TIP ♥
These can be made 2–3 days in advance and wrapped in clear film (plastic wrap). They can be hung for a few days, but after that the sweets (candies) will begin to soften.

1 Preheat the oven to 180°C/350°F/ Gas 4. Line a large baking sheet with some non-stick baking parchment. Make a window template (see back of book). Thinly roll half the gingerbread mixture on a floured surface. Cut out windows using the template and transfer them to the baking sheet. Re-roll the trimmings with the remaining dough and make more windows. Use a metal skewer to make a hole in the top of each cookie. Bake the windows for 5 minutes.

2 Meanwhile, very lightly crush the boiled sweets by tapping them firmly, still in their wrappers, with the end of a rolling pin.

3 Remove the half-baked cookies from the oven and place a few pieces of crushed sweet in each section of the windows. (You will need about two sweets per window.) Return the cookies to the oven and bake for a further 5 minutes, until the sweets have melted to fill the windows. Re-make the skewer holes, as the gingerbread will have spread a little during baking. Leave the windows on the baking sheet to cool.

4 Thread a length of fine ribbon or string through the hole of each window, to hang them.

GLAZED GINGERBREAD COOKIES

The quantity you can make of these little cookies will depend on the size of the cutters you use. They also make good hanging cookies, for decorating trees and garlands. For this, make holes in the cookie with a skewer, and thread with fine ribbon.

MAKES ABOUT 20
1 quantity Golden
Gingerbread mixture
2 quantities Icing Glaze
red and green food colourings
175g/6oz white almond paste

1 Preheat the oven to 180°C/350°F/ Gas 4. Grease a large baking sheet. Roll out the gingerbread dough on a floured surface and, using a selection of cookie cutters, cut out a variety of shapes, such as trees, stars, crescents and bells. Transfer the cookies to the baking sheet and bake for 8–10 minutes, until they are just beginning to colour around the edges.

2 Leave on the baking sheet for 2 minutes and then transfer to a wire rack and leave to cool. Place the wire rack over a large tray or plate to catch the drips. Using a dessert-spoon, spoon the icing glaze over the cookies until they are completely covered. Leave in a cool place to dry for several hours.

3 Knead red food colouring into one half of the almond paste and green into the other half. Roll a thin length of each coloured paste and then twist the two together into a rope. Secure a rope of paste around a cookie, dampening the icing with a little water, if necessary, to hold the paste in place. Repeat on about half the cookies.

4 Dilute a little of each food colouring with water. Using a fine paintbrush, paint festive decorations over the plain cookies. Leave to dry and then wrap in tissue paper.

CHRISTMAS TREE PLAQUES

M ake plenty of these pretty cookies and combine them with festive bows to hang on a tree that will need little other decoration.

MAKES 12
1 quantity Golden
Gingerbread mixture
1 quantity Royal Icing
green and blue food colourings
lemon juice
silver dragees
fine ribbon

♥ COOK'S TIP ♥
*You will need fine ribbon or string
to thread these cookies.
Alternatively, loop thicker ribbon
through the spaces over the heads of
the gingerbread figures.*

1 Preheat the oven to 180°C/350°F/ Gas 4. Grease two large baking sheets. Roll out the gingerbread dough on a floured surface and cut out gingerbread figures, using an 8cm/3¼in cutter. Space them well apart on the baking sheets.

2 Re-roll the trimmings and cut them into strips, 1cm/½in wide and 28cm/11in long. Position a strip around one figure, so that the ends meet over the head and the curved edge just meets the limbs. Repeat with each of the remaining figures.

3 Use a skewer to make a hanging hole in the top of the outer frame. Bake the cookies for about 12–15 minutes. Leave on the baking sheets for 3 minutes and then transfer to a wire rack to cool.

4 Put a little of the royal icing in a paper piping bag fitted with a writing nozzle. Divide the remaining icing into two bowls. Colour one half green and the other blue. Use a little lemon juice to thin the consistency of each, until the icing thinly coats the back of a spoon. Using the writing nozzle, pipe lines of white icing across the hands, feet and collars of the figures. Also draw on a face.

5 Spoon a little coloured icing on to the body, spreading it to the edges using a cocktail stick (toothpick). Use the rest of the coloured icing to coat the remainder. Secure a row of dragee 'buttons', pushing them into a line with the tip of a skewer. Leave to set for 2 hours. Decorate the edges with white icing piping, securing dragees with dots of icing. Thread the cookies with ribbon for hanging.

CHRISTMAS COTTAGE

This cottage is built using a very basic 'house' shape, but the Christmas snow theme gives it a very pretty, dreamy finish. The piped windows and doors should be left to harden for one or two days, so you might prefer to make these first.

*2 quantities Golden
Gingerbread mixture
1 quantity Royal Icing
28cm/11in round cake board
675g/1¹/₂lb white sugar paste
icing (confectioners') sugar, for dusting
25g/1oz black sugar paste
25g/1oz red sugar paste
25g/1oz green sugar paste*

1 Preheat the oven to 180°C/350°F/ Gas 4. Grease two baking sheets. From paper, cut out two 20 x 11cm/ 8 x 4¹/₄in rectangles for the cottage roof. Cut two rectangles measuring 19 x 9cm/7¹/₂ x 3¹/₂in for the front and back. On the front, cut two 3 x 2cm/ 1¹/₄ x ³/₄in windows and a small door. Cut two further windows on the back. For the sides, draw a 9cm/3¹/₂in square on to paper and add a pointed gable on one side, which measures 7.5cm/3in from the point to the base of the roof. Cut out two sides, adding a window in each.

2 Roll out the gingerbread dough and cut out all the templates. Transfer the gingerbread shapes to the baking sheets and bake for 15 minutes, until they are just beginning to colour around the edges. Leave on the baking sheets for 3 minutes and then transfer to a wire rack to cool.

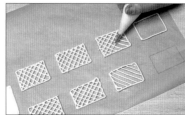

3 On a large sheet of non-stick baking parchment, draw seven 4 x 3cm/1¹/₂ x 1¹/₄in rectangles. Mark one 6 x 5cm/2¹/₂ x 2in rectangle. Put a little of the royal icing into a paper piping bag fitted with a large writing nozzle. Pipe over the marked outlines on the paper. For the windows, pipe diagonal lines across the small rectangles and then across in the opposite direction. (One window is spare, in case of breakage!) Fill in the larger rectangle with lines of piping for the door. Leave to harden for 24–48 hours in a cool place.

4 Brush the cake board lightly with water. Roll out 225g/8oz of the sugar paste on a surface dusted with icing sugar and use it to cover the board, trimming off the excess around the edges. Put more royal icing in a paper piping bag and cut off the tip. Pipe a line of icing down one short side and stick it at right angles to a side section on the iced board.

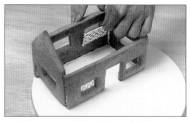

5 Pipe more icing along the base on the inside. Secure the back and remaining side sections in the same way. Peel the lining paper away from the windows. Pipe a little icing around the edges of the windows and stick them in place. Secure the door in the same way. Leave to harden for 1–2 hours in a cool place.

6 Pipe more icing over the top edges of the cottage and secure the roof sections. Spread a little icing over the roof area. Roll out another 350g/12oz of the white sugar paste to a 20cm/8in square. Lift it over the roof, so that it covers the gingerbread. Neaten the edges of the sugar paste.

7 Using a thin nozzle, drizzle bits of icing down from the roof to look like icicles. Use the black sugar paste to shape small window sills and a door knob. Secure with a little icing. Lightly knead a dot of the black sugar paste with a little of the white until marbled. Break off small pieces and flatten them into 'stones' for the path. From the remaining white sugar paste, shape small cones for trees and secure with a dampened paintbrush. Roll a little red and green sugar paste as thinly as possible. Twist into ropes and use to decorate the front door and some of the trees. Lightly dust the house with icing sugar.

♥ *COOK'S TIP* ♥
Once the sugar paste is in place on the cottage roof, you may find it easier to trim the edges with a pair of sharp scissors than with a knife. Mould the paste over the edges of the gingerbread to look like thick snow.

TEMPLATES

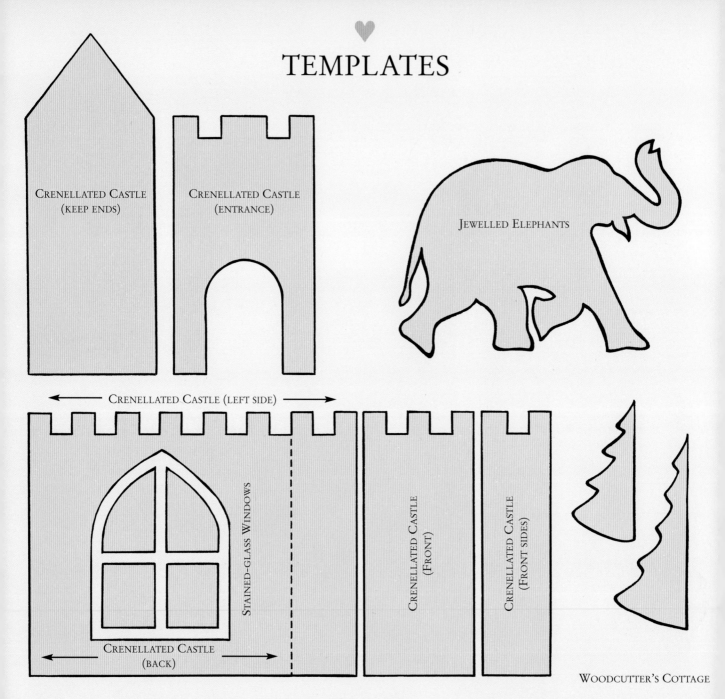

Crenellated Castle
(KEEP ENDS)

Crenellated Castle
(ENTRANCE)

Jewelled Elephants

◄——— Crenellated Castle (LEFT SIDE) ———►

Stained-glass Windows

Crenellated Castle
(FRONT)

Crenellated Castle
(FRONT SIDES)

◄——— Crenellated Castle
(BACK) ———►

Woodcutter's Cottage

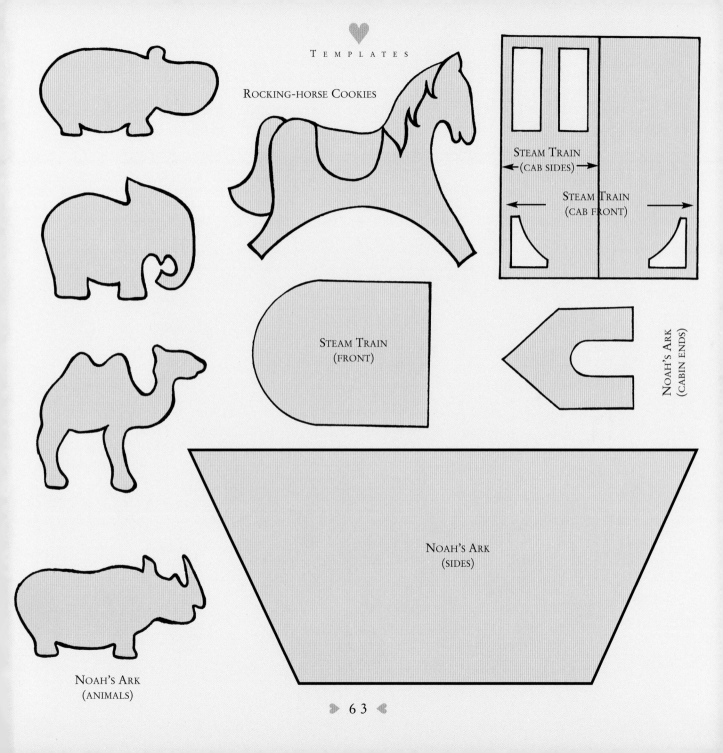

TEMPLATES

ROCKING-HORSE COOKIES

STEAM TRAIN
← (CAB SIDES) →

STEAM TRAIN
← (CAB FRONT) →

STEAM TRAIN
(FRONT)

NOAH'S ARK
(CABIN ENDS)

NOAH'S ARK
(SIDES)

NOAH'S ARK
(ANIMALS)

INDEX